The Power
of
Connection

Maximize Your Health and Happiness with Close Relationships

GREGORY L. JANTZ, PHD
WITH KEITH WALL

AspirePress

Contents

Created *to* Connect

Think back to your high school literature class, and you might recall reading the famous 1624 poem by English writer John Donne, who penned, "No man is an island, entire of itself; every man is a piece of the continent, a part of the main."

Donne's words emphasize that no one can thrive alone, cut off from other people. Human beings are social creatures, in need of close connection with others.

This is the way God designed us! In the first pages of Scripture, God declared that people were not intended to live solitary lives: "It is not good for the man to be alone" (Genesis 2:18). Human beings were created to participate in community, forge lasting bonds with each other, help one another, and share life experiences. Alone, we wither; together, we bloom.

Because close relationships are so vital to our healthy functioning, concerned experts have been sounding the alarm that chronic loneliness has reached epidemic levels in modern society. A 2020 large-scale report released by health-service company Cigna showed that America's loneliness epidemic is worsening. Three out of five adults (61 percent) report they are lonely—a 7 percent increase from 2018.[1]

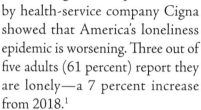

HUMAN BEINGS ARE SOCIAL CREATURES, IN NEED OF CLOSE CONNECTION WITH OTHERS.

Loneliness does not merely mean the lack of friends. People with many friends can still feel socially detached, just as those with few friends may rarely or never feel a sense of separation.

What's more, being alone doesn't necessarily mean being lonely, nor is it always something negative. Some people, particularly introverts, enjoy time by themselves and are quite comfortable with solitude. Even extroverts desire "me time" to reflect and recharge.

Loneliness is different. When we're lonely, we're alone—but not by choice, leading to feelings of sadness or emptiness. We may feel cut off or alienated from other people and have no one we can genuinely communicate with. Even when we're surrounded by others, we can still feel alone if we don't have a connection with them.

We all need people with whom we can share our innermost thoughts and feelings: People who will laugh with us during joyful times and cry with us during painful times. People with whom we can experience the unfolding of daily life—through all the ups and downs.

In the pages ahead, we'll explore the many advantages of connection with others, the disadvantages of disconnection, the ways modern-day society contributes to isolation, and the specific ways you can form healthy bonds with new people and deepen your existing relationships.

ALONE, WE WITHER; TOGETHER, WE BLOOM.

You'll discover that the payoff for pursuing human interaction is well worth the investment, with the rewards being greater health, well-being, resilience, purpose, spirituality, and enjoyment of life. You'll hear this message from scientists and researchers who have backed up that claim with real data, and from people like you whose stories constitute a different kind of evidence. In fact, firsthand testimony may be the most powerful persuader of all, because it can provide a pivotal ingredient, without which we won't get far in our quest for reconnection—encouragement that it really is *possible* to reverse recent trends toward social isolation, fragmentation, and widespread loneliness, and to claim a happier life.

Together we will explore the secrets of genuine togetherness so we can heal our wounds, find comfort in each other, and build a healthier future, both individually and as a society. If you are willing to take some risks, invest in the process, and expand your skill set, you'll find yourself empowered to deeply engage with others. Your relationships will flourish, as will your entire life!

The Key *to* Connection

Before moving on, it's worth pausing to look at a couple of key points that will deepen our understanding.

First, what matters most to health and well-being is the *quality* of our relationships. This conversation about connection is in no way meant to justify staying stuck in toxic or abusive circumstances. Those kinds of relationships work against wellness. For instance, research shows that a healthy marriage can contribute to a feeling of emotional support, but an unhealthy one can create stress, compromise a person's immune system and endocrine function, and play a part in depression.[2]

WHAT MATTERS MOST TO HEALTH AND WELL-BEING IS THE *QUALITY* OF OUR RELATIONSHIPS.

Marriage is by no means the only kind of relationship that can become a source of stress. Toxic behavior can be found in just about any setting—school, work, church, family, and so-called friendships. My purpose in pointing this out is to be certain we avoid the mistaken conclusion that any relationship is better than none. Far from it! If you are in a harmful

or life-draining situation, learning the positive benefits of healthy connection may well provide you with hope that a better life is available—and with the motivation you need to work toward it. (To better understand the impact of unhealthy relationships—and the value of healthy ones—see my book *How to Deal with Toxic People*.)

TRUE ENGAGEMENT WITH OTHER PEOPLE HAPPENS ON THE *INSIDE*, IN YOUR MIND AND IN YOUR HEART.

The second important idea to grasp is that true engagement with other people happens on the *inside*, in your mind and in your heart. In other words, even if circumstances separate you physically from the people close to you, it is still possible to maintain the kind of connection that delivers all the benefits I'll present in this book.

Reaping the rewards of close relationships often requires a different mindset and a measure of determination and creativity, but it is *always* well worth the effort!

CHAPTER 1

The Problem *of* Disconnection *and the* Power *of* Connection

Healthy people are growing people, and people do not grow healthy in isolation. We need each other for many reasons, including companionship, encouragement, support, feedback, and guidance. Because of this, the character of people we surround ourselves with, and strive to form deep connections with, matters tremendously. We can't always select the people who fill our lives, but in most cases we *can* choose those we get close to. Moreover, we can choose to form relationships with people who share the desire to develop a stronger bond with others.

Think for a moment about the people whose company you value and cherish; recall those who make a difference in your life for the positive. They are interested and invested in you. They share their lives with you and encourage you to do the same. They pick you up when you fall. They strive to bring out the best in you. They accept you for who you are and challenge you to pursue your goals with energy and determination.

Such relationships are essential for healthy emotional, social, and spiritual development. Unfortunately, developing and maintaining these needed interconnections is becoming an increasing struggle as our culture shifts. Loneliness has been a mounting concern for decades, with some level of isolation now afflicting millions of people in North America. In his groundbreaking book *Bowling Alone* (2000), Robert Putnam documented the growing alienation experienced by Americans as previously vibrant aspects of society that fostered togetherness, such as bowling leagues, faded away. The close-knit fabric of communities began to fray, and people retreated indoors, often not even knowing the names of those who lived around them.

HEALTHY PEOPLE ARE GROWING PEOPLE.

More recent research shows that loneliness was worsening prior to the COVID-19 pandemic. In 2018, a joint Kaiser Family Foundation and *Economist* survey found that one in five Americans "often" or "always" felt lonely or socially isolated.[3]

THE CHARACTER OF PEOPLE WE SURROUND OURSELVES WITH MATTERS TREMENDOUSLY.

According to a study published in February 2021 by Harvard University's Making Caring Common project, loneliness is defined as "the negative feelings that emerge from a perceived gap between one's desired and actual relationships." The study found that 36 percent of respondents felt lonely "frequently" or "almost all the time or all the time."[4] In this report, researchers point out the broad reach of isolation:

> Loneliness also doesn't seem to spare any major demographic group. Among our survey respondents, there were no significant differences in rates of loneliness based on race or ethnicity, gender, level of education, income, religion, or urbanicity. Large numbers of survey respondents in both political parties suffer loneliness, although Democratic respondents were more likely to report loneliness (40%) than Republicans (29%).[5]

A similar study Cigna conducted in 2019—before the COVID-19 pandemic—supports these conclusions, but startlingly identifies significant generational differences in loneliness. The findings revealed that younger generations are dramatically more lonely than older people. Nearly eight in ten Gen Z members (79 percent) and seven in ten Millennials (71 percent) are lonely, compared to only 50 percent of Baby Boomers.[6]

The High Cost of Loneliness

Even before pandemic-related social disruptions came along, researchers widely viewed loneliness as an epidemic with serious health implications. Although measuring feelings can be subjective, taking stock of the effects of those emotions is not. Much research supports the conclusion that loneliness contributes to health risks, including:

- Depression and anxiety
- Substance-abuse disorders
- Suicidal thoughts
- Aggressive behavior and impulsivity
- Cognitive decline
- Obesity

- Cardiovascular problems

- Diminished immunity

- Sleep disruption

- Premature mortality[7]

The Harvard report referenced earlier echoes this association, citing evidence to support the stunning claim that "lacking social connection carries the same if not greater health risks as heavy smoking, drinking, and obesity."

ISOLATION AND LONELINESS ARE *SERIOUS* PROBLEMS WITH REAL AND OFTEN DEVASTATING CONSEQUENCES.

My purpose in presenting these troubling statistics is to firmly lay this foundation: Isolation and loneliness are *serious* problems with real and often devastating consequences, as in the case of increased suicide risk. The ramifications deeply affect everyone in our society in one way or another and should not be taken lightly.

But here's the good news: This is a problem with an attainable solution, an ailment with an achievable cure. Let's explore an example drawn from composites of real-life stories, and then we'll dig into what we can do to regain the full, healthy, and powerfully united life God intends for us!

A Study *in* Contrasts

Imagine you've just parked in the lot of a well-maintained suburban apartment complex. You step out of the car and follow the winding sidewalk past lush landscaping and an inviting swimming pool and fitness center. Ahead is a staircase leading to the upper stories of Building C.

You climb to the first landing and stop. To your right and left are two identical apartment doors, except for the metal numbers affixed to the outside.

Anita

Go through the door to your right and you'll meet Anita, age twenty-eight. No life is without its hard knocks, but Anita seems somehow more resilient than most when challenges arise. She works at home as a bookkeeper, specializing in helping small-business entrepreneurs start off on the right financial footing.

Technically, Anita works alone. In reality, she feels surrounded by friends all day because she makes a point of getting to know her clients by more than the contents of their spreadsheets. Any time she has reason to talk with them on the phone, the conversation begins with a recap of personal news. A couple of times each summer she hosts a client appreciation barbecue in the park to socialize with them in person.

Though Anita's parents and siblings live in another city, they talk frequently online and by phone. In addition, she belongs to an informal group of other single women who serve as her social and emotional support system. They've become her book club, cooking circle, car maintenance co-op, and night-on-the-town posse. When she's not spending her spare time with "the girls," Anita can usually be found at the gym or a green-space trail around her neighborhood.

Christy

In the apartment next door lives Christy, age thirty-three, who also resides alone. She manages a nearby popular coffee shop and bakery. Unlike Anita, Christy spends her days around crowds of people, but those relationships are all professional and mostly superficial. She considers it inappropriate to form friendships with people she supervises, and she purposely limits contact with customers, preferring the relative quiet behind the kitchen doors. At home, Christy spends most of her time online—shopping, playing games, or interacting with social media. She eats mostly microwave-ready meals and struggles with a variety of chronic physical and mental health issues, including headaches, persistent fatigue, insomnia, and depression.

The Bigger Picture

One of these people is generally happy and thriving, and the other is not.

These two women and their stories are composites compiled from the experiences of dozens of people, male and female, whom I've had the privilege to counsel over the years. The contrast I've drawn between their respective lifestyles is an oversimplification; in the realm of health and well-being, it is never possible to attribute complex conditions and circumstances to a single influence or choice. We are each the product of interactions among multiple forces pulling and pushing us through our lives. What is possible to recognize, however, are the patterns and consistencies at work in the big picture that are useful for arriving at helpful and healing conclusions.

With that in mind, here's what Anita and Christy, and many men and women like them, have taught me through the years: Genuine, healthy connection with other people is a key ingredient in creating a happy, purposeful, and fulfilled life.

Studies seeking to identify the root causes of a wide range of mental and physical disorders—up to and including suicidal thoughts or plans—have repeatedly pointed toward isolation as a major risk factor. It is a clear warning sign when someone suddenly (or chronically) shuns contact with others and drops off the radar. Every list of positive steps a person can take to address problems with anxiety, depression, addiction, and thoughts of self-harm includes advice related to maintaining connection with others and avoiding isolation.

GENUINE, HEALTHY CONNECTION WITH OTHER PEOPLE IS A KEY INGREDIENT IN CREATING A HAPPY, PURPOSEFUL, AND FULFILLED LIFE.

"But wait," I've heard so many people say. "How can spending time around other people be a solution when my past dealings with *people* have been nothing but painful—and even traumatic!"

Finding a way around this conundrum is what this book aims to do. If you keep reading, you will find answers to questions such as, *Why does engaging with others matter? How can I find meaningful relationships in a culture that is so often isolating and individualistic?*

What's more, we'll discover that genuine connection with each other is key to living up to the ideal the apostle Paul set for us:

> As God's chosen people, holy and dearly loved, clothe yourselves with compassion, kindness, humility, gentleness and patience. Bear with each other and forgive one another if any of you has a grievance against someone. Forgive as the Lord forgave you. And over all these virtues put on love, which binds them all together in perfect unity. (Colossians 3:12–14)

These standards for godly living are not possible if we live in compartmentalized bubbles that intersect only superficially, if at all. Thankfully, since in many cases remaining isolated and disconnected involves choices we make every day, we can always make new choices that enable us to develop genuine, intimate, life-giving relationships!

What Do We Mean *by* Connection?

What do I mean when using this word? Perhaps we might discover what true human connection *is* by thinking about what it is *not*. For this, it's helpful to look back at the story of Anita and Christy.

Connection Is Not Just about Being Together

Being physically close to people is certainly preferable in any relationship. Research indicates that between 70 to 93 percent of human communication is nonverbal.[8] We convey how we feel through facial expressions, tone of voice, body language (such as crossed arms or stiff posture), eye contact, and more. We're much more attuned to those cues when we're face-to-face. But recall that Anita spends the bulk of her day by herself as a self-employed bookkeeper, while Christy is surrounded by people at the bakery she manages. Simply being near others is no guarantee of connection, while circumstances that require physical solitude don't automatically doom you to isolation.

Connection Is Not to Be Confused with Networking

Some researchers claim that a larger number of weak-tie acquaintances is better for increasing opportunity in life than a handful of strong ties. As one *Psychology Today* contributor put it, "Strong ties make the world smaller; weak ties make it bigger."[9]

Fair enough, and that's certainly one way to interpret Anita's efforts to engage with her clients. But the writer goes on to acknowledge, "A bigger world may mean a world with more opportunities, but it goes without

GENUINE ENGAGEMENT IS A MATTER OF *QUALITY*, NOT *QUANTITY*.

saying that economic gain is not the only standard by which to judge a potential relationship."

So true! Which is why Anita went the extra step and cultivated strong ties with friends outside work as well.

Connection Is Not Measured by Friends or Followers on Social Media

Christy spends hours each evening reading and making posts online, while Anita rarely has time to keep up with the few social media contacts she has. Connection is not a numbers game. As we'll see in a moment, genuine engagement is a matter of *quality*, not *quantity*.

Connection Is Not a Noun but a Verb—a Purposeful Action on Our Part

Anita takes the initiative in getting to know her clients better. She is interested enough to ask meaningful questions and then actively listen to the answers— which leads her to more questions. She spends time, energy, and other resources organizing periodic picnics and hikes.

FOUR CONDITIONS FOR CONNECTION

Definitions of what constitutes a close relationship vary, but key ingredients include shared experiences, mutual interests, togetherness, emotional connection, and support in times of need.[10] True connection grows between people who are

1 **Available to each other**—tangibly, emotionally, philosophically, and spiritually;

2 **Truly present**—not only as a matter of proximity but also in the sense of being undistracted, caring, able to really listen, and ready to help;

3 **Nourishing and supportive**—connected people lift each other up with consistent encouragement; and

4 **Willing to be genuine**—openness and vulnerability, though not always easy to achieve, draw two people together emotionally.

What Do We Mean *by* Isolation?

Having laid that groundwork, it is much simpler to define the opposite of connection: *isolation*. This word characterizes the withering state that develops when people are unavailable to each other because of selfishness or unresolved trauma, anger, fear, or guilt; an unhealthy and imbalanced belief that every-person-for-themselves competition is necessary for survival in the world; and even a genetic predisposition toward the loner personality type. However, isolation can also stem from other causes, such as illness, disability, or advanced age that keeps someone housebound or separated from others.

> "LET US CONSIDER HOW WE MAY SPUR ONE ANOTHER ON TOWARD LOVE AND GOOD DEEDS, NOT GIVING UP MEETING TOGETHER, AS SOME ARE IN THE HABIT OF DOING, BUT ENCOURAGING ONE ANOTHER."
>
> –Hebrews 10:24-25

Throughout the ages, loneliness has been the subject of poets, authors, and musicians who have used powerful imagery to express this universal emotion. In the song "I Am a Rock," Paul Simon uses stark terms that allow listeners to see clearly the tragedy of choosing isolation over healthy social interaction.

It's true that well-defined and maintained boundaries are a necessary part of mental and emotional health and well-being. But a person who is socially isolated has turned those boundaries into an impenetrable wall, making beneficial attachment difficult, if not impossible.

IT IS EVERY BIT AS POSSIBLE TO FEEL DESPERATELY ALONE IN A CROWDED ROOM AS IT IS ON A DESERTED ISLAND.

As was true of connection, isolation isn't only about *where* you are. It is every bit as possible to feel desperately alone in a crowded room as it is on a deserted island. Lacking the ability to connect, the isolated person may come to feel they *are* that island.

But it's not just about connecting— the *type* of link we forge with others is vitally significant.

Are All Connections Created Equal?

Returning once more to the Harvard study, its authors observe,

> Loneliness is a bellwether not only of our country's emotional and physical but moral health. In this age of hyper-individualism, the degree to which

Americans have prioritized self-concerns and self-advancement and demoted concern for others in many communities has left many Americans stranded and disconnected. We need to return to an idea that was central to our founding and is at the heart of many great religious traditions: We have commitments to ourselves, but we also have vital commitments to each other, including to those who are vulnerable.[11]

"Commitments to each other," in this context, is a pivotal concept that explains why casual connection is not enough to dispel crippling loneliness. Commitment implies investment in *quality* over *quantity*.

YOUR SOCIAL EXPERIENCES CAN DIFFER SIGNIFICANTLY DEPENDING ON WHOM YOU SPEND TIME WITH.

As recounted in the bestselling book *Thrive*, National Geographic Society researcher Dan Buettner set out to discover why people in some regions of the world score consistently high in surveys designed to measure overall happiness. What do those communities get right, he wondered, that the rest of us could learn from? Not surprisingly, greater social connection ranks high among his findings.

But as we've seen already, the link is not a simple matter of how often one gets out of the house to be around other people or how many so-called friends one maintains on social media. Nor is it true that all social interactions—even those quite close and personal—are created equal. Your social experiences can differ significantly depending on whom you spend time with. Buettner writes,

> Who we hang out with has an enormous and measurable influence not only on how happy we are, but also on how fat we are, or even how lonely we are. On any given Tuesday night, we can sit in a bar and listen to an old acquaintance's problems, or we can spend that evening going to the theater with an upbeat friend. According to one statistical analysis, each additional happy friend we have in our social circle boosts our cheeriness by nine percent, while each additional unhappy friend drags it down by seven percent.[12]

As we move on to further explore why connection matters so much, what its absence means for the world, and how to create more of it in our lives, keep in mind that this is not a call to be *busier*. Our aim is to be genuinely *better* together, and more available to each other. It's an invitation to nurture relationships in which we can shine forth qualities the apostle Paul called us to exemplify: compassion, kindness, humility, gentleness, patience, and love. It's an opportunity to reach out to our neighbors and extend ourselves when we see a need, rather than turning away or withdrawing. To choose to become part of the fabric of our community as we experience a shared journey through life. To give—and receive—grace and forgiveness, and experience fulfillment and blessing as we use our God-given skills and talents in serving others. It's a call to foster soul-enriching relationships in whatever corner of the world God has placed us so we can live more fully and abundantly.

That's connection worth having!

> "DO NOT LET ANY UNWHOLESOME TALK COME OUT OF YOUR MOUTHS, BUT ONLY WHAT IS HELPFUL FOR BUILDING OTHERS UP ACCORDING TO THEIR NEEDS, THAT IT MAY BENEFIT THOSE WHO LISTEN. . . . GET RID OF ALL BITTERNESS, RAGE AND ANGER, BRAWLING AND SLANDER, ALONG WITH EVERY KIND OF MALICE. BE KIND AND COMPASSIONATE TO ONE ANOTHER, FORGIVING EACH OTHER, JUST AS IN CHRIST GOD FORGAVE YOU."
>
> –Ephesians 4:29, 31-32

CHAPTER 2

Why Connection Is Worth *the* Effort

During the COVID-19 pandemic, Sammy and Donald, both in their late 70s, discovered how vital social relationships are, and how worthwhile it is to maintain them. For years, the men had met every Friday morning in a neighborhood coffee shop for espresso and a game of chess. The game board between them was a figurative campfire that they gathered around each week to tell stories, share news, listen to each other, and laugh. Coffee shop baristas always looked forward to the infectious sound of their camaraderie.

Then COVID-19 arrived.

"I'll never forget standing on the sidewalk outside the cafe one morning, with the chess set tucked under my arm, trying to make sense of the sign taped to the door,"

Donald recalled. "The sign said, 'Closed until further notice.' It felt like a death in the family."

In response, both men retreated into their respective homes, where they each lived alone. Being part of the at-risk population, social isolation and self-protection seemed to make sense. As time went on, however, even their brief phone calls began to seem "socially distanced" and strained by fear—becoming shorter and fewer.

"It came as a real shock to realize one morning," said Donald, "that I felt truly *lonely*. Honestly, it made me mad to think my story might end like Mozart's—sad and alone."

Rewriting *the* Story

Suddenly Donald remembered he wasn't simply a victim of events. He could rewrite the story himself. So he made a plan. Step one: Figure out how to use Zoom, the video teleconferencing software program he'd heard about. Step two: Get online and order two espresso machines, one for himself and the other to be delivered to Sammy. Step three: Set up the chessboard where his computer camera could see it—and call his friend with a challenge.

"That's how the Virtual Coffee Shop and Chess Club was born," Sammy told me with a smile. "I think it saved my life to figure out that we didn't have to stop laughing and being friends just because we couldn't actually be together."

Sammy and Donald remained in touch through challenging times—and even strengthened their friendship—because they *chose* to, and then worked at it. The connection they created wasn't dependent on proximity. It lived inside them, fueled by desire and determination.

The bottom line: God intends for you to have nothing less than a rich, purposeful, and connected life, no matter what obstacles might arise in the world. You begin to do your part when you believe that's possible—and take steps to make it happen.

With that in mind, we're ready to tally up the dividends that greater social connection will pay to anyone who invests in it.

GOD INTENDS FOR YOU TO HAVE NOTHING LESS THAN A RICH, PURPOSEFUL, AND CONNECTED LIFE, NO MATTER WHAT OBSTACLES MIGHT ARISE IN THE WORLD.

■ ■ ■

Connection *and the* Body

In the world of scientific research, not a shred of doubt remains that relationships with others are good for your physical health.

At age forty-seven, Cheryl suffered relatively minor injuries in a car crash—multiple contusions on her head and chest, a broken wrist, strained back muscles, and several cracked ribs. None of those issues gave her doctors cause for alarm, however, and they told her that with rest and light physical therapy she could expect a full and quick recovery. In addition, they advised her to lose twenty-five pounds and stop smoking, and based on Cheryl's answers to the standard mental health survey that primary care providers routinely administer, her physician referred her to a counselor for consultation and prescribed antidepressant medication to "help her get over the hump." It was a reasonable treatment plan.

RELATIONSHIPS WITH OTHERS ARE GOOD FOR YOUR PHYSICAL HEALTH.

Except it didn't work.

"I was in terrible pain all the time, and the meds they gave me didn't even make a dent," Cheryl said. "I could barely move. The physical therapy that was supposed to help was just torture."

Worse Becomes Worst

Then she developed a respiratory infection that led to pneumonia. Three weeks after the accident, Cheryl was back in the hospital in worse condition than on the day of the crash. Her blood work showed evidence of a sluggish and suppressed immune response and a variety of other imbalances that puzzled the doctors. What didn't show up in any of the tests was the fact that, in addition to suffering from her physical condition, Cheryl was desperately lonely.

For several months before her accident—since the conclusion of a painful divorce—she'd been sinking deeper and deeper into social isolation. Her ex-husband had been emotionally and psychologically abusive, but the breakup strained her other relationships, as many of her friends and family were unable to see the truth of the abuse for themselves. Her days now consisted of nothing but time spent at work and time alone at home.

The extra weight the doctors advised her to lose and the smoking they told her to quit were recent developments in Cheryl's life, along with her struggles with mental health issues. Several days of medical intervention in the hospital stabilized her condition enough to justify sending her home again—but did nothing to address the chronic illnesses resulting from isolation and loneliness.

Genuine Connection

Fortunately, a neighbor in Cheryl's apartment building was up to that task. Jeanette recognized distress when she saw it, even in fleeting moments of casual contact. That's because she had been down the road of desperation herself, as a US Army veteran who came home after two tours in Iraq with severe post-traumatic stress disorder. From her own treatments, she knew firsthand two things that would prove to be pivotal in Cheryl's recovery—from her injuries *and* the trauma of her divorce:

> First, Jeanette knew that loneliness is not just a state of mind. It holds serious consequences for physical health as well. Second, genuine connection with others is a powerful tonic, able to reverse the damage done by isolation.

Jeanette shared with Cheryl that taking the first step to reach out to others can be difficult, like having to take a bad-tasting medicine. "You might have to make yourself take it at first," Jeanette told Cheryl, "but if you do, you won't be sorry."

Specifically, Jeanette prescribed an unlikely treatment that had worked for her: joining an improv comedy troupe. Though the group performed regularly to appreciative audiences around the city, its real purpose was therapy for PTSD patients.

GENUINE CONNECTION WITH OTHERS IS A POWERFUL TONIC, ABLE TO REVERSE THE DAMAGE DONE BY ISOLATION.

"Jeanette had to push me there—literally, because I was in a wheelchair!" Cheryl recalls. "I spent the first hour determined to hate it. But after a while I couldn't help myself and started laughing. That turned into tears, and it was

like some logjam of pain inside broke. Those people gathered around me and, just like that, became my new family."

True Healing

As her new relationships blossomed over the next few weeks, Cheryl's recovery got back on track. She committed to a weight loss and nutrition program, signed up for a nicotine patch treatment system, and reconnected with friends she'd temporarily lost through her divorce.

"I can't imagine where I'd have wound up without Jeanette," Cheryl admitted. "It's too dark to think about."

Though it's tempting to credit this inspiring story to some X factor that made Cheryl more resilient than most people after receiving a little boost, mountains of research suggest there is far more to it than that. Scientists have concluded, in fact, that social connection produces more than an improved outlook on life; it also results in tangible, measurable physical effects within the human body that play a direct role in our ability to heal.

How Does Connection Help Us Heal?

One surprising answer might be found in the research of Steven Cole, a professor of medicine at UCLA. Cole and his colleagues wondered if the link between loneliness and disease—and conversely between social connection and health—might actually be found in our DNA. Could certain genes express themselves differently under different social circumstances? The answer, he discovered, is yes. His findings, in fact, have launched an emerging field of study called social genetics.

Cole found that human genes behave differently in lonely people than in those who don't identify as feeling detached from others. Specifically, genes that govern how the immune system works show consistent up-regulated inflammatory gene expression and down-regulated antiviral response.[13] In other words, people experiencing loneliness suffer from more inflammation and a compromised immune system. Furthermore, Cole suspects that loneliness and gene expression may play off each other—that is, loneliness has a negative effect on gene behavior, which in turn fosters increased feelings of separation.

With this stunning discovery, Cole has found at least one tangible explanation to support what other researchers have observed for decades—socially active people experience better health and longer life expectancy than people who isolate themselves. In fact, Cole's landmark paper, which is a survey of the existing body of research on the link between social connection and health, lists several remarkable conclusions:

- Social relationships have significant effects on health.

- Social relationships affect health through behavioral, psychosocial, and physiological pathways.

- Relationships have costs and benefits for health.

- Relationships shape health outcomes throughout the life course and have a cumulative impact on health over time.

Clearly, maintaining solid social connection with others pays off with broad-spectrum health benefits—up to and including how long we can expect to live. A Harvard University report states, "One study, which examined data from more than 309,000 people, found that lack of strong relationships increased the risk of premature death from all causes by 50 %—an effect on mortality risk roughly comparable to smoking up to 15 cigarettes a day, and greater than obesity and physical inactivity."[14]

Thankfully, these deadly health risks are reversible—when we commit to finding and maintaining healthy relationships.

Connection *and the* Mind

We've just seen how powerfully our physical health is influenced by positive relationships, and the same is true for our mental health. In fact, neuroscientists specifically use the word *reward* to describe what happens when a person participates in overtly social behavior. This reward takes the form of neurochemicals that are produced by the body and linked to our ability to experience happiness and well-being. Research over several decades has firmly implicated that when natural processes are imbalanced or disrupted, these chemicals act as culprits in depression and other mental disorders.

SOCIALLY ACTIVE PEOPLE EXPERIENCE BETTER HEALTH AND LONGER LIFE EXPECTANCY THAN PEOPLE WHO ISOLATE THEMSELVES.

By peering into the inner workings of the body, modern researchers have added another benefit to that list—our predecessors were also *happier*. We now know that isn't just a subjective value judgment. Social connectedness literally boosts a sense of mental and emotional well-being by stimulating the body's production of dopamine, serotonin, and oxytocin—the chemicals that antidepressant medications attempt to regulate. Social isolation, by contrast, suppresses the process and contributes to a negative feedback loop in which one condition only makes the other worse.

Connection *and* Resilience

In the 1993 Walt Disney Pictures version of Alexandre Dumas's *The Three Musketeers*, the young swordsman d'Artagnan hopes to follow in his father's footsteps to become a musketeer in service to the king. Throughout the film, he is pursued by men who want revenge for some perceived offense. He narrowly escapes them time and again. After the story's climax, when d'Artagnan finally wears the blue cloak of a musketeer, the men catch up to him, and a showdown seems inevitable. Not yet used to his new place in the community of fellow musketeers, d'Artagnan says to his brothers, "I'll handle this" and moves to meet his accusers alone.

Porthos takes him by the arm and reminds him, "D'Artagnan, 'All for one and one for all.'"

Then all the musketeers draw their swords. The film ends with d'Artagnan's accusers fleeing in front of a veritable tidal wave of blue cloaks in pursuit.

This image is a fun illustration of one benefit of social connection that is harder to quantify but no less powerful than the others. It's about having backup in time of need—or having people who will show up to the party when there is something to celebrate.

Cheryl's Story

Think back to Cheryl's story. By facing her divorce and then her injuries alone, she left herself in a depleted physical and mental state. Not only were her immune system and recuperative powers compromised, but she was also on shakier mental footing, and her choices regarding overeating and smoking reflected that. In addition, being isolated from others meant she lacked any practical help just getting by.

"For months I'd been driving with windshield wipers that made a muddy mess when it rained," Cheryl said. "I'm not mechanically inclined to begin with, but I also didn't have the energy or the basic ability to focus."

Even after making new friends, she felt stuck and unable to deal with such a simple repair. Then it occurred to her: One member of her new "family" had been a vehicle mechanic in the military. Once she got up the courage to approach him, she discovered he was delighted at the chance to help. In fifteen minutes, the problem was solved.

Notice something important: This is exactly the kind of social interaction that researchers have discovered can trigger a release of dopamine and other helpful chemicals in the body. "All for one and one for all" is far more than a catchy phrase; it is a social philosophy that triggers all sorts of positive benefit in our lives.

Connection *and the* Meaning *of* Life

"Why am I on earth? Does my life really matter? What's my purpose for being here?"

Who hasn't asked these questions at some point and struggled to find satisfying answers?

Like generations of philosophers before us, we are likely to be disappointed if we expect to find a single, definitive answer to these questions. The search for meaning is one that each of us has to undertake, and no one but you can fill in the blanks about your specific purpose as you listen and look for God's guidance.

Still, this doesn't mean we can't spot what is generally true about human life and glean wisdom from it. The very fact that the search for purpose is universal throughout history tells us there must also be something that permeates all the possible answers.

In my decades of experience as a mental health professional, I've seen repeatedly how the healthy search for meaning in life morphs into something darker for someone who struggles with depression. The question, "Why am I here?" gets twisted into, "What does it matter whether I'm here or not?"

I trust you can see and feel the difference. One question is hopeful, curious, and open to adventure; the other is focused inward and oriented toward limitation, lack, and hopelessness. The former is the outlook of someone actively engaged with the world; the latter of a person who has withdrawn from it and from other people. As we have seen, God designed the human body to tangibly reward social activities that put interaction with others at the center of our lives. Modern society seems determined to do the opposite, fostering isolation and increasingly extreme "me-centric" pursuits—creating a disaster for human health and well-being.

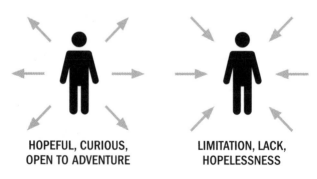

HOPEFUL, CURIOUS, OPEN TO ADVENTURE

LIMITATION, LACK, HOPELESSNESS

Living in Reciprocity

Now let's go a step further and acknowledge that it isn't simple interaction with others that helps define our reason for being on earth. If it did, then a trip to the mall would feel rejuvenating instead of draining, as it so often is for many people. Real purpose is found in something else that's embodied in what many might call an old-fashioned word: *service*. In other words, to paraphrase a popular Albert Schweitzer quote, "The only really happy people are those who have learned how to serve."

I believe this is true, for reasons that go directly to the heart of all we've said so far about the benefits of living in connection with others—and the dangers of not doing so. But allow me to further paraphrase Schweitzer's statement and refine the concept of service:

> The only really happy people are those who have learned to live in reciprocity with others.

The act of serving—although a kind deed—can still be done without meaningful engagement. You might sort donated clothes at the homeless shelter without interacting with anyone. Sorting clothes is a benefit to a worthwhile cause but not interpersonally enriching for you. Or you might consider it a service to write a monthly check to a favorite charity—a worthy endeavor, but one that falls far short of the kind of social connection we're talking about here.

To live in reciprocity with others means being available to both give and receive. When you are part of a community of people, you'll do both. You will give as you can; and you'll let someone else do the same for you when the need arises. In this sense, real service can only be accomplished when you are connected.

Could it be that our relationships with others intertwines with our purpose? I believe the answer is yes! This does not mean that service must be an undertaking of epic proportions. The young man who changed Cheryl's windshield wipers was just as firmly rooted in his life's purpose in that moment as someone delivering relief supplies to refugees in a remote corner of the world. The power and proof are not in the scale of the action, but in the depth and integrity of your connection with another person.

Even the smallest act of kindness can have tremendous significance. When we sacrifice time or money or choose to do the right thing even when it's not convenient, not only does it benefit the person we reach out to, but we receive blessing and encouragement as well. That's because we're acting in obedience to God's commands.

God Will Respond

Scripture is packed with examples of people taking risks—giving in sacrificial ways even when they can least afford it or stepping out in faith into an unknown future. Reaching out to others or getting involved within your community might not be easy—or even what you feel like doing, especially if you're struggling with feelings of rejection, isolation, or loneliness. But remember that time and again in the Bible, when people acted with love, courage, and obedience, God responded by pouring out his blessing, power, and faithful provision.

In the story of the widow's offering in Mark 12:41–44, Jesus watched people putting money into the temple treasury. Those who were rich gave large amounts and made a great show. But when Jesus observed a woman giving only two small copper coins, he said, "This poor widow has put more into the treasury than all the others. They all gave out of their wealth; but she, out of her poverty, put in everything—all she had to live on" (vv. 43–44).

In God's economy, the heart motive is what matters, and he blesses us when we respond in obedience to what he's asked us to do, whether the request seems small or great in our eyes. As Matthew 25:40 says, "Truly I tell you, whatever you did for one of the least of these brothers and sisters of mine, you did for me."

Connection *and* Spiritual Practice

The spiritual leaders of Jesus' day often tried to trap him in some contradiction in his teaching so that they could use it against him. Here's an example:

> One of them, an expert in the law, tested him with this question: "Teacher, which is the greatest commandment in the Law?" Jesus replied: "'Love the Lord your God with all your heart and with all your soul and with all your mind.' This is the first and greatest commandment." (Matthew 22:35–38)

What a marvelous and elegant answer! It points to an extremely worthy and rewarding way to spend our lives: loving our Creator without reservation or limitation, focusing all our attention on him and the experience of communion together. Sometimes this pursuit is best served by periods of meditative solitude—those mountaintop moments that people of faith often seek at organized church retreats or in camp settings. Jesus himself was known to spend time alone in the wilderness, withdrawn from others, to pray, listen, and recharge.

Love Your Neighbor as Yourself

My own experiences of spiritual solitude have generally come to a jarring end when I must leave the mountain and return to the hustle of daily life. *Why can't I stay in that tranquil, peaceful state forever?* I've wondered.

One answer is found in the second half of Jesus' answer to those questioning him: "And the second [commandment] is like it: 'Love your neighbor as yourself.' All the Law and the Prophets hang on these two commandments" (vv. 39–40).

Here's where these commandments have relevance in our conversation about the rewards of connecting with others. You see, it is theoretically possible for the avowed hermit to fulfill the first half of Jesus' instruction to "love the Lord your God." But what of the second? Can we really love our neighbors as ourselves if we isolate ourselves from contact with them? In some abstract sense, perhaps it counts to simply wish the best for people from a distance. But that certainly seems to fall short of what the apostle Paul advised about real love between people:

> "MAY THE LORD MAKE YOUR LOVE INCREASE AND OVERFLOW FOR EACH OTHER AND FOR EVERYONE ELSE, JUST AS OURS DOES FOR YOU."
>
> –1 Thessalonians 3:12

> Love is patient, love is kind. It does not envy, it does not boast, it is not proud. It does not

dishonor others, it is not self-seeking, it is not easily angered, it keeps no record of wrongs. Love does not delight in evil but rejoices with the truth. It always protects, always trusts, always hopes, always perseveres. (1 Corinthians 13:4–7)

Those inspiring qualities are meaningless in isolation. To obey the second-greatest commandment positively requires *connection with others*. But here's the best part: Everything we've learned about the benefits of interpersonal relationships means this commandment is no burden or call to sacrifice; it's a recipe for healthy, happy, wholesome living! "Love your neighbor as yourself" might also be taken to mean that loving your neighbor *is* loving yourself—by closing the circuit of social connection to everyone's benefit.

Mother Teresa once said, "The most terrible poverty is loneliness and the feeling of being unloved." We might add that the feeling of having no one to love is just as painful.

Loving connection is the healing salve that soothes both.

CHAPTER 3

Identifying Causes *of* Disconnection

Loneliness not only affects greater numbers of people than ever before but also affects them more deeply and fundamentally. Separation hurts—emotionally, physically, mentally, and spiritually.

Rarely does loneliness suddenly pop up in one's psyche. Usually isolation is part of a downward spiral that begins with withdrawal from whatever connectedness you once had with a person or group. If unchecked, the spiral can plunge you into sadness, depression, and despair.

▼ WITHDRAWAL

Withdrawal from social connection may be voluntary or involuntary. You may decide to unfriend or block a social-media contact (voluntary) or someone may unfriend or block you (involuntary). You may feel ignored or devalued by a boss or peer group. A personal friendship may languish from inattention or disagreement, or you might stop attending a coffee klatch or a church group or an exercise class for whatever reason. Without remedy, withdrawal can lead to . . .

▼ SOCIAL ISOLATION

Though we all experienced a degree of social isolation during the COVID-19 public health emergency, we're not talking about quarantines here. (Though isolation may feel like it.) We're addressing a voluntary separation from others and the normal verbal and nonverbal interactions that are crucial to one's emotional health and well-being.

As we discussed earlier, God created people to be together, not alone. He established that you and I were designed to be involved in meaningful, caring relationships. Without significant interconnectedness with others, we're prone to . . .

▼ LONELINESS

We've all felt lonely at one time or another, and it's not pleasant. One client of mine described the feeling as a "bottomless heartache." People might have casual interactions with coworkers and acquaintances, but an underlying lack of deeper friendships gnaws at the soul.

Isolation is a condition many people have a hard time breaking free from. "Loneliness causes people to feel empty, alone, and unwanted," says author and educator Kendra Cherry. "People who are lonely often crave human contact, but their state of mind makes it more difficult to form connections with other people. . . . Loneliness, according to many experts, is not necessarily about being alone. Instead, if you *feel* alone and isolated, then that is how loneliness plays into your state of mind."[15]

And prolonged loneliness can easily lead to . . .

▼ DEPRESSION

Depression has many causes, and if you struggle in this area, I strongly advise seeing your physician and a qualified counselor. Social isolation and loneliness can generate feelings of emotional and physical lethargy, hopelessness, and worthlessness—classic symptoms of clinical depression. Tragically, when you are depressed and in greatest need of contact with people, that is also when you least feel like being with them. Which only drives you to ...

▼ DEEPER ISOLATION

What if you *do* reach out to others but don't feel embraced by them? The tendency is to retreat further. Deeper isolation may feel safer temporarily—that is, if you're not connecting with someone, you're protecting yourself from rejection.

But deeper isolation only feeds the feelings of separation and depression you're already struggling with. By now, if you haven't stopped the vicious cycle, your deeper isolation could become ...

▼ DESPAIR

You don't want to sink this far. Despair is near the very bottom of the downward spiral and is a precursor to suicidal thoughts or actions. Despair lies to you—it whispers that no one likes you or wants to be with you, that you're no good anyway, that you have no purpose or reason for being, that the hurt will only go away if you do.

I can confidently assure you that such negative voices are not from God, for he is the giver of life and purpose. He created you and placed you in this world for a reason. He loves and values you so much that, as author Max Lucado so wonderfully writes in his book *Traveling Light*, "The maker of the stars would rather die for you than live without you."[16]

So please do not give heed to the lying voices of despair. Seek help immediately from your pastor, doctor, or counselor.

Causes *of* Isolation

Because I don't want to see you anywhere near the vicious downward spiral we've just examined, it's important to be aware of how our modern-day life promotes isolation and works against meaningful connection. By understanding the *causes* of personal withdrawal and isolation, we can better remain vigilant against these detrimental tendencies—while strengthening the emotional, social, and spiritual foundations of healthy, fulfilling interactions. Some reasons for isolation include the following:

1. Poor Health and Disabilities

Some people who are embarrassed by their disabilities or health problems might isolate themselves to avoid social interaction, fearing they will be judged, stigmatized, or considered a burden. Other people might struggle with mobility issues due to physical limitations, making it more of an effort to get out and socialize with others.

2. Pandemics

We all remember what COVID-19 did—and in many ways continues to do—to our social lives! Who can forget the months of closed schools, restaurants, churches, and businesses? We endured extended periods of empty concert and sports venues, social distancing, masks, and fears and disputes over whether to vaccinate or not. In many ways, disconnection and isolation were mandated during the pandemic ... and it was inevitable that a sense of separation would follow.

3. Busyness and Overactivity

Constant busyness often gives the impression (to ourselves and others) of a robust social life and an abundance of relationships. But jam-packed schedules often preclude the unhurried time and slow rhythms needed to develop intimacy and trust with others. Commotion does not equal connection.

4. An Unhealthy Emphasis on Self-Reliance

Overemphasis on self-sufficiency and autonomy leads many people to believe they don't need others—or at least to be reluctant to seek help when it's needed. Especially in American culture, people celebrate and strive for rugged individualism and independence. Asking for help and relying on others can be seen as a weakness, but needing companionship and closeness is not the same as being needy.

5. Misuse or Abuse of Technology

But as much as we need close relationships, concerned experts have been sounding the alarm that chronic loneliness has reached epidemic levels in modern society. As Harvard Medical School professors Jacqueline Olds and Richard Schwartz point out in their book *The Lonely American: Drifting Apart in the Twenty-First Century,*

> Over the last decade, the debate about freedom and connection in the United States has leaped from rarely read doctoral dissertations to front-page national news. What caught people's attention was a series of alarms, given in the form of data-driven studies, suggesting that our society is in the midst of a dramatic and progressive slide toward disconnection.[17]

6. Substance Abuse and Other Addictions

Addiction can be both a cause and a result of isolation. Many times this problem coincides with mood-related disorders, but loneliness can also be a cause. With substance abuse rates at an all-time recorded high, this is a significant factor for social isolation.

7. Unemployment

If someone resigns or is fired, dismissed, or released from a job and struggles to find work for a long period of time, their sense of self-doubt, unworthiness, and insecurity can worsen into isolation and loneliness. When the unemployment rate goes up, social isolation rates also rise.

8. Aging

Due to problems such as cognitive impairments and disabilities, older people may be unable to go out and socialize, or they are often less confident in doing so.

9. Loss of a Spouse

If someone has recently endured a separation, a divorce, or the death of their spouse, he or she may feel lonely and depressed. Meanwhile, friends may feel uncomfortable reaching out, not knowing what to say or not say.

10. Societal Adversity

Some people simply don't want to deal with the hassles and headaches that come with a stressed, competitive, and impolite society. What sociologists call *societal adversity* can create a desire to avoid the discomfort, dangers, and responsibilities of being around people who are rude, hostile, judgmental, crude, or otherwise unpleasant. People on the receiving end of mistreatment sometimes choose to avoid others as much as possible, keeping to themselves as a protective or defensive measure. And we can't mention societal adversity without addressing a more recent ugly trend . . .

11. A Culture of Divisiveness

It used to be that, for the most part, people knew how to disagree agreeably. Even when differences of opinion or disputes arose, people were likely to treat each other with civility and respect. Nowadays, news and social media can contribute to divisiveness and polarization, with individuals sometimes responding in inflammatory ways against those whose opinions don't conform to their own. In an environment of division and hostility, some people choose to remain silent and maintain a safe distance from others. Genuine communication and authentic sharing of feelings may be stunted when there is fear of being harshly criticized or excluded.

Social Media *and* Disconnection

Perhaps the most ironic modern-day cause of withdrawal, isolation, and even depression comes via social media.

On the One Hand . . .

Granted, when used responsibly and in moderation, social media makes life easier and better. It can provide

- consistent connection and communication with friends and family;

- reduced feelings of isolation among the elderly;

- opportunities to promote a small business or organization;

- awareness and fundraising to support a worthy cause; and

- tools for spreading vital information during an emergency.

But on the Other Hand . . .

As we've seen, *misuse* of technology and social media can be anything but social. Used unwisely or without discernment, they can be instruments of hatred, hostility, misinformation, and exclusion.

But even when we keep things civil, technology and social media can be *overused*. You see it wherever you go . . .

1. Men and women, teens, and even children sit staring at the cell phones in their hands.

2. People cluster in groups but are transfixed by their tiny screens.

3. Drivers attempt to steer multi-ton vehicles while texting, endangering their passengers as well as other drivers.

4. Grown men and women walk the hallways at work, glued to their phone screens, failing to make eye contact or to just say hi as they cross paths with coworkers.

5. We've all seen groups of friends or whole families dining together in restaurants, forgoing in-person conversation to stare silently at their cell phones.

Indeed, a growing body of research makes it clearer every year that social media use has a dark side— including the elevated risk of withdrawal, isolation, and depression. The dangers posed by excessive or imbalanced use of social media include

■ decreased verbal and nonverbal communication skills;

- decreased in-person interaction;

- literal endangerment due to distraction;

- increased isolation;

- an increased sense of loneliness;

- a distorted sense of reality due to misinformation and censorship;

- connection addiction and FOMO—the Fear of Missing Out;

- lower self-esteem and "comparison anxiety";

- a false sense of intimacy;

- cyber-bullying; and

- virtual cancellation, which declares you and your opinion unworthy of public attention.

Young people are more likely to be impacted by the negative effect of social media interaction on mental health and well-being. Compounding matters, young people tend to be especially dependent on both social media and peer norms and approval, making them particularly vulnerable to social media's harms, including the production of false selves, the deluge of people enjoying others' company, and ostracism and bullying.[18]

IF SOCIAL MEDIA ACTS AS A SUBSTITUTE FOR IN-PERSON RELATIONSHIPS, A PERSON'S SENSE OF ISOLATION AND INADEQUACY CAN WORSEN.

When considering the link between loneliness and social media use, studies show that the way in which a person uses social media is significant. Using technology to maintain or develop new friendships through Facebook, Snapchat, Instagram, TikTok, or other apps can help certain relationships flourish. However, if social media acts as a substitute for in-person relationships, a person's sense of isolation and inadequacy can worsen.[19]

Based on many years of working in the mental health field, I can confirm from firsthand experience that the misuse and overuse of technology have a direct impact on the severity of isolative and depressive symptoms. In fact, at our clinic and in my writing and speaking, social media misuse/overuse has become a regular part of diagnostic work with troubled clients of all ages.

Real Connection, Real People

While the Internet or social media may provide helpful information and communication forums with friends and family, it is counterproductive to rely on technology for meaningful friendship. Good people are out there, and they want and need positive friendships as much as you do. So take the risk: Put down your electronic devices and initiate getting involved with others and nurturing friendships. Options are almost limitless! Join a gardening or chess club, participate in a painting night, try an exercise or cooking class. Activities exist for any area of interest you have—including both active and passive recreation. Whether you like being indoors or outdoors, with large groups or small groups, opportunities to connect with people abound!

REDISCOVER THE FULFILLMENT OF MEANINGFUL CONNECTION.

Sometimes it takes courage to get out of your comfort zone and try a new activity or develop new relationships. You might not necessarily even *want* to do these things at first. But don't shy away from new relationships or experiences because you feel daunted by the possibility of embarrassment or failure or simply fear of the unknown.

It's time to get over withdrawal, break free of isolation, kiss loneliness goodbye—and rediscover the fulfillment of meaningful connection.

Connect with Yourself First

To paraphrase Carl Jung, the grandfather of psychology: Loneliness doesn't come from being alone; it comes from not being able to communicate about the things that matter. He was breaking new ground in the early 1900s, and his words hold true today.

In our modern era, we have countless methods of communicating and an ever-growing social group. Why, then, do so many people report feeling isolated, lonely, and depressed? Perhaps the key isn't communicating more or differently with others but how we attempt to communicate and reconnect with *ourselves*.

Following are three ways to listen to your loneliness and an explanation of why it's a worthwhile endeavor:

1. **Have an honest conversation—with yourself.** Loneliness is a sign that we have been neglecting our own needs. When was the last time you checked in with yourself? We spend so much of our time outwardly focused that it's easy to overlook our own needs. Neglecting yourself will only intensify your sense of separation. How can anyone else know your needs if you don't? To get back in touch with yourself, start by journaling about your biggest disappointments, your deepest yearnings, and your greatest hopes for the next three months. You

might be surprised at what you discover about yourself in the process.

2. **Explore your spiritual side.** Spirituality is perhaps the most overlooked aspect of health. While the mental aspect of health is enjoying its rightful moment in the sun, spirituality often remains ignored. We are created for communion with others. Our lives have meaning and a God-directed purpose designed to play out in the arena of our connection with others—our homes, families, communities, religious organizations, places of work, and wherever else life takes us.

> "MOST IMPORTANT OF ALL, CONTINUE TO SHOW DEEP LOVE FOR EACH OTHER, FOR LOVE COVERS A MULTITUDE OF SINS. CHEERFULLY SHARE YOUR HOME WITH THOSE WHO NEED A MEAL OR A PLACE TO STAY. GOD HAS GIVEN EACH OF YOU A GIFT FROM HIS GREAT VARIETY OF SPIRITUAL GIFTS. USE THEM WELL TO SERVE ONE ANOTHER."
>
> –1 Peter 4:8–10 NLT

For lack of a thriving spiritual life, many of us attempt to create meaning by pursuing activities that will ultimately not bring fulfillment. Again, this topic makes for a great journaling prompt. What has your spiritual journey up to this moment looked like? What have you appreciated, what would you like to retain, and what would you like to change moving into the future? What do you have to offer in friendships and other relationships? Answering these questions will help fill your "spiritual needs" bucket.

3. **Examine how your lifestyle might be reinforcing loneliness.**
Your individual health and the health of your relationships are determined almost completely by the choices you make, moment by moment and day by day. In the preceding pages, we've discussed many of the ways our modern culture contributes to loneliness and isolation. But we are not helpless and defenseless against the forces that surround us. We can choose to use technology wisely. We can choose to regulate our schedule to allow breathing room. Set aside time to assess your daily routine and choices—and see how you might be contributing to your own sense of disconnection.

WE ARE CREATED FOR COMMUNION WITH OTHERS.

Loneliness is healed when we foster a stronger, healthier relationship with ourselves. And that's a relationship guaranteed to last. Once we understand ourselves well and recognize the sources of our feelings of separation, we're in an excellent position to develop connections with other people by adopting attitudes and actions that will propel us forward. In the next section, we'll explore many ways to form deeper and richer relationships.

CHAPTER 4

Fostering Deeper Connections

Throughout the previous year, Jack had struggled with feelings of deep depression, lack of energy, and low self-esteem. His beloved wife of twenty-five years had died of cancer, leaving Jack to finish raising their two teenage daughters by himself. He had invested his time, energy, and love into these girls, who felt sorrow at the loss of their mother and confused by the usual struggles of adolescence.

Jack's single-parenting efforts were exceptional, helping his two daughters to eventually become well-adjusted young women. In turn, each of them went off to college far from home, a proud accomplishment for Dad and daughters. But Jack suddenly found himself an empty nester. Worse, he was a *single* empty nester, living alone in a house that seemed painfully silent every second of every day.

Bored with his work as an accountant and lacking any meaningful involvements, Jack had sunk deeper and deeper into withdrawal and isolation. He spent almost every evening in front of the TV, often with a bottle of wine beside him, slowly draining it before nodding off in his recliner. His poor physical health and lifestyle habits contributed greatly to his poor mental health. Jack slept fitfully almost every night, ate microwavable meals, and spent countless hours aimlessly surfing the Internet when he wasn't watching TV.

Alone, unmotivated, and disoriented by many painful transitions, Jack felt worthless and hopeless. He saw little reason to keep trying at life and had contemplated suicide more than once. Thankfully, his sister—one of the few people he communicated with—insisted that he seek professional help. Resistant for a long time, Jack eventually gave in to her persistent persuasion and scheduled an appointment for counseling at the clinic I direct.

| Making *a* Plan

My team and I counseled Jack on multiple fronts. A first-step strategy we used with him seemed obvious but turned out to be a powerful one: Start reengaging with the world! Reach out to old friends who have drifted away. Identify one or two people who might become new friends. Say hello when he happens to be outside and sees neighbors walking their dogs. Find an activity to join—a cooking class, a sports league, a walking group—and identify a church or faith-oriented group to get involved with.

"You don't have to do all of this at once," I told Jack. "Start small and begin rebuilding your connections with others. It won't happen overnight, but you will eventually find your life full of meaningful relationships—if you will be intentional about your choices."

Working together, Jack and I created a "prescription" for an action he would take each week, a practical step to talk with or spend time with others.

Positive Results

Slowly but surely, over several weeks, Jack's efforts started to pay off. He summoned his energy and courage to talk with a few people on the phone and then invite them to meet for coffee. He began walking with a neighbor several mornings each week. Then he signed up for a ceramics class at the local arts center. None of this was easy for him, as he had well-established patterns of keeping to himself. He had admirably raised his daughters but all the while ignored his own needs.

As Jack's social life improved, so did his mental and emotional life. Though still weighed down by depression, he began to feel glimmers of hope that he could regain the joy and meaning in life that had been sorely lacking.

Did Jack's intentional plan to form connections with others cause his depression to completely go away? No, of course not. There were other important issues he needed to address with the help of professionals: his poor eating habits, excessive drinking, lack of exercise, unresolved anger, and grief he had not processed. He had plenty of work to do to restore stability to his mental health. But moving out of loneliness and into connectedness was a significant component in his recovery, and he was finding people who would encourage and support him as he worked to achieve well-being.

I hasten to add that there are no magic formulas for overcoming mental health struggles—no easy-to-follow plan that will provide instant healing for a person's emotional troubles. However, I am convinced of the life-changing power of committing to specific actions and attitudes that promote physical, emotional, spiritual, and mental health.

Solid Steps *toward* Connection

You might recognize themes in Jack's story that are present in your own life. Or your personal situation may be quite different. But there's little doubt you are seeking deeper connection with others—otherwise you would not be holding this book in your hands.

Perhaps you, like so many people, have no one in your life you can call a true, close, intimate friend. Or maybe you have a number of shallow relationships you want to deepen into something more authentic. Or possibly you want ideas to move your friendships from good to great. Whatever your situation, let me offer five keys to connection for initiating new relationships and seventeen strategies for deepening existing ones.

FIVE KEYS TO CONNECTION

When entering into any kind of gathering, seek to:

1 **Find common ground.** Connection happens when you discover a shared interest, be it golf, travel, or Humphrey Bogart movies.

2 **Show sincere interest.** Develop a real desire to know more about the person you're with. Make it your mission to truly listen and understand.

3 **Self-disclose.** Openness begets openness. Emotional connection happens when two people reveal important information about themselves.

4 **Encourage authenticity.** Allow the person you're with to be free to be who they are—total openness with no judgment.

5 **Find the hidden treasure.** Everyone has an aspect of life that is their greatest source of joy—their children, the screenplay they're writing, the mentoring program where they volunteer. Discover the other person's passion, and share in the enthusiasm.

1. Step Out of Your Comfort Zone and Take Risks

Some people have no problem meeting, greeting, and forming new relationships. Others have a much tougher time. They must summon their courage, swallow their anxiety, and plunge into social settings.

TAKING RISKS MEANS CHOOSING COURAGE OVER CAUTION.

If you tend to be reserved and restrained, there's no point in trying to remake yourself into an outgoing, life-of-the-party type. Be who you are—but be prepared to push yourself.

Taking risks means choosing courage over caution. When it comes to deepening relationships, we all have our reasons for hesitating. Perhaps you've been burned before and have learned to shy away from risk. Maybe you are immobilized by a thousand scary what-ifs.

Whatever the case, notice where those reasons all reside: in the past or future, but rarely in the present. Courage can't cope with everything that has ever caused you pain or might hurt you in the future, but it can easily overcome what is present right now. The bottom line: In this moment, there is little to lose and everything to gain.

2. Put Yourself in the Company of a Variety of People

It could be a small-group Bible study, support group, community project, book club, or exercise class. But choose something to join, and do it now. There's a saying that you can't get to second base with one foot on first. It's the same challenge you face in drawing closer to others. Move away from your past isolation and get involved at the basic level with other people. Even if you do not participate fully in an event, have the courage to be present.

You can't learn to swim by reading a book about swimming, and you will never achieve closeness with others unless you take the risk of being in their presence.

3. Show Respect at All Times

Mutual respect is at the core of close relationships. It confers dignity, honor, and high worth to the recipient. In contrast, lack of respect leads to all kinds of relational ills—put-downs, dishonesty, neglect—which are sure to sink a relationship eventually.

MUTUAL RESPECT IS AT THE CORE OF CLOSE RELATIONSHIPS.

Part of showing respect means honoring differences. People's view of the world and how to live in it may not be the same as yours due to their life experience, temperament, personality, upbringing, and access to education. Once you sincerely strive to understand these differences, you automatically feel more compassion and acceptance.

When you accept, you don't judge; when you stop judging, people start responding to you and connecting with you.

4. Prove Your Reliability

We all let things fall through the cracks now and then. We forget a friend's birthday, show up late for an important meeting, or misplace the car keys. It happens. But this can start to be a real problem when it becomes chronic flakiness. While these people often have enjoyable personalities—optimistic, spontaneous, and playful—they are also extremely frustrating for those who rely on them to complete a task or show up on time.

For a relationship to enjoy a deep connection, both people must act responsibly. They need to keep their word and honor commitments. If you tell your friend, "I'll read the book you gave me," you should do it and respond with feedback. If you say, "I'll come help you move on Saturday morning at 9:00," you should follow through exactly as you promised. If one or both people are consistently negligent, the relationship is sure to suffer.

> "RELIABLE FRIENDS WHO DO WHAT THEY SAY ARE LIKE COOL DRINKS IN SWELTERING HEAT—REFRESHING!"
>
> –Proverbs 25:13 MSG

As psychologist David Niven says, "With all the complicated advice available about relationships, sometimes the basics can be overlooked. Relationships depend on communication; we all know that. And meaningful communication demands reliability. Your words need to mean something. Say what you mean, and do what you say you are going to do. Always. If you do, you will have taken a huge step toward positive communication and a positive relationship."[20]

5. Emphasize Empathy

You know the old saying, "Don't judge someone unless you've walked a mile in their shoes." That adage is a simplified version of what empathy means: You try to put yourself in the other person's position. You try to understand what they are feeling. You try to experience their world as best you can.

Mutual empathy is a powerful connector that is made possible by mirror neurons in our brains. Mirror neurons act like an emotional Wi-Fi system. When we feel the emotions of others, it makes them feel connected to us. When we feel their positive emotions, it enhances the positive emotions they feel. When we feel their pain, it diminishes the pain they feel. If someone expresses emotion, it's helpful and honoring for you to feel it too.

6. Let Grace and Kindness Flow out of You

The most beautiful people in the world have an inner warmth and generous spirit that spills onto those around them. We can't resist drawing near to someone who is consistently gentle, compassionate, and accepting. These straight-from-the-heart qualities more than compensate for any shortcomings a person might have.

To put this principle into practice, you can

- send a handwritten note to someone you know is struggling—or for no particular reason;

- call a friend or acquaintance out of the blue to say, "I want you to know how much I appreciate you"; or

- give a coworker, neighbor, or teacher an unexpected gift, such as a latte, muffins, or a candle; the gift itself doesn't matter nearly as much as the generosity behind it.

7. Give Compliments Generously

It seems so simple and yet is often overlooked: A genuine compliment offered at the right time, in the right way, can help a relationship move to a new level of closeness. Why? Because we're all human, and we all love to know we are appreciated and admired.

Millennia ago, King Solomon wrote thousands of proverbs that offer guidance and insight. Recognized by historians as one of the wisest people who ever lived, he said, "Gracious words are a honeycomb, sweet to the soul and healing to the bones" and "A word fitly spoken is like apples of gold in a setting of silver" (Proverbs 16:24; 25:11 NRSV).

Those were poetic ways of saying that words of affirmation and approval have a dynamic effect on the recipient. In this regard, nothing has changed since the ancient days of Solomon: Inspirational words will resonate and reverberate in the life of the one who receives them.

OUR FEELINGS FOR ANOTHER PERSON ARE STRONGLY INFLUENCED BY HOW THAT INDIVIDUAL MAKES US FEEL ABOUT OURSELVES.

8. Help Other People Feel Good about Themselves

Psychologists have identified a secret to wonderful relationships: Our feelings for another person are strongly influenced by how that individual makes us feel about

ourselves. Since one of the most potent motivations in life is to feel good about ourselves, we will be drawn to people who do just that.

Some may say this principle sounds self-centered and egocentric, but it is a basic fact of human nature and can be a powerful positive force. People who feel the closest connection are the ones who support, praise, and strengthen each other. As the apostle Paul urged in 1 Thessalonians 5:11, "Encourage one another and build each other up, just as in fact you are doing."

9. Master the Art of Listening

When you listen, you'll learn things that will help you appreciate the other person more deeply. You'll catch a glimpse of his or her hopes and dreams, hurts and fears. You'll discover new ideas and thoughts. If you're not in the habit of listening—*really* listening—you'll miss all these things and more.

Sadly, many people think of listening during a conversation as simply waiting for their turn to speak again. But there is great power in the practice of paying deep and focused attention to what another person has to say. We should listen to hear, not to formulate a response before we've even absorbed the person's words.

Everyone wants to be heard and seen, but in a world dominated by the white noise of constant communication and information, it rarely happens. This is an unfortunate social reality, but it offers you the opportunity to distinguish yourself from the self-absorbed and distracted crowd by the simple act of listening well.

Even among people who grasp the importance of effective communication, listening well is an endangered skill. The key ingredient is simple: focus. Here's how:

- Don't let distractions compromise your concentration. Find a quiet place to talk. Turn off your phone. Set aside all devices that might lure your attention.

- Maintain eye contact. Looking the other person in the eye demonstrates that you are engaged and interested.

- Pay close attention to what is being said. Repeat what you heard the other person say in your own words.

- Emphasize empathy. Convey that you "get" what the other person is saying and you identify with his or her feelings.

- Be a "role model." Verbalize your own thoughts and feelings, and then allow plenty of space for the other person to do the same.

- Accentuate affirmation. Anytime someone makes the effort to be transparent with you, let him or her know you appreciate it.

10. Ask Questions—Lots of Them

Curiosity may have killed the proverbial cat, but the lack of it will murder your mastery of connection. Think of yourself as a reporter on assignment. But you don't want the typical small talk facts: "Where are you from?" and "What do you do?"; instead, you're after the story behind the story. You can delve deeper by asking questions like

- Who has been the biggest influence on your life?

- What was your family like growing up?

- What were you like as a kid?

- What kinds of things really make you laugh?

- What's your favorite place in the entire world?

- Who is your best friend? What do you like about him/her?

- What's your biggest goal in life right now?

- Have you figured out your calling in life? What is it?

Nothing engages people faster than meeting someone who is genuinely interested in them. Listen closely to the other person's response to your question—and then ask follow-up questions such as, "Can you tell me more about that? Was that hard for you? What did you do after that?" Doing so will demonstrate interest in the speaker's point of view. This reveals that you're listening closely and want to know more. Asking questions can eliminate uncomfortable small talk and help you get into more meaningful conversations.

11. When Communicating, Strive for Equal Time

Some people consider themselves skilled communicators because they can talk endlessly. But the ability to speak is only one part of the equation, and not the most important. Communication requires talking *and* listening.

The best communication occurs with an even and equal exchange between two people. Think of communication as the two oars that propel a rowboat. If only one oar is churning the water, you will find yourself going in circles. If neither oar is moving, you're dead in the water. Two oars moving in rhythm will keep you moving steadily forward. Similarly, great communication occurs as each person alternately talks and listens, talks and listens.

THE BEST COMMUNICATION OCCURS WITH AN EVEN AND EQUAL EXCHANGE BETWEEN TWO PEOPLE.

If you're not someone who is a natural conversationalist, don't feel daunted thinking there must always be a fifty-fifty exchange of dialogue. Social interaction and the art of communication are skills you can develop. Even if you never feel 100 percent comfortable, with practice you can project confidence and hold your own in social settings.

12. Be Supportive of the Other Person's Goals and Dreams

Everyone has aspirations they would like to see come to fruition. It might be a health-related goal like losing weight or stopping smoking, or a career goal like achieving a promotion or starting a business. It could be a family goal related to kids or parents, a goal of helping others, or even a long-held dream of writing a book, visiting a foreign land, or running a marathon.

> "BE KIND AND COMPASSIONATE TO ONE ANOTHER, FORGIVING EACH OTHER, JUST AS IN CHRIST GOD FORGAVE YOU."
>
> –Ephesians 4:32

By lending a listening ear, offering encouragement, brainstorming together, or helping to conduct research, you communicate an important message: "Your dreams and ambitions are important to me, just as they are to you."

13. Be Real

The key to satisfying relationships is recognizing that perfection is never a requirement for worth and value. Don't hide your imperfections. Let them become apparent—and then strive for self-improvement.

Accept your shortcomings and realize that everyone has areas that need work. Cut yourself some slack—

and while you're at it, cut others slack too. In any relationship between friends, family members, or coworkers, the person who gains a clear perspective on herself or himself is always viewed as the healthiest, the most attractive, and the one others want to be around.

These people create an atmosphere of honesty and acceptance. They are thoroughly accepting of others just as they are. Since they can admit their deficiencies, they make it possible for others to deal openly with their own struggles and problems. Because they do not present themselves as flawless, they remove the pressure for others to live up to impossible standards.

Work on developing a gracious and understanding spirit toward those around you. As Paul admonishes in Ephesians 4:32, "Be kind and compassionate to one another, forgiving each other, just as in Christ God forgave you."

Those who are highly accepting are highly attractive. We love to be around people we know aren't judging our worth and evaluating us to see if we measure up. If you want to develop deep connection with others, be a person who is accepting and gracious. Accept your own faults and foibles—and extend this same grace to those closest to you.

14. Serve Others and Serve Together

There's something magical about the connections we build when we give without expecting anything in return. Loneliness often diminishes when we devote ourselves to serving others. Perhaps that's because serving others increases our self-esteem, something no other person can do for us. So challenge yourself to care for people who can't repay you. Check into volunteer opportunities in your community. Do good to feel good.

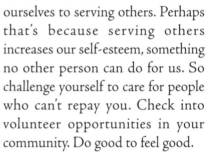

IN ALL COMMUNICATION, TILT HEAVILY IN THE DIRECTION OF COMPLIMENTS OVER CRITICISM.

Another aspect of this principle involves serving alongside another person. Research shows that people who work together in acts of ministry or service develop respect, appreciation, and admiration for one another. When you care for others—feeding the homeless downtown alongside your friend or shoveling your elderly neighbor's sidewalk—you create new possibilities for relating.

By serving together and feeling great about it, you increase the positive thoughts you have toward the person you're with and create new memories together.

15. Resist the Urge to Criticize

Nobody likes to have their faults and flaws pointed out. Unless something has become destructive to your friend or is causing a significant problem between the two of you, suppress the urge to say something negative. In all communication, tilt heavily in the direction of compliments over criticism.

If you absolutely must offer constructive criticism, do so with much grace and gentleness. Think about how you'd want someone to approach you if the situation were reversed.

16. Be Eager to Forgive

No matter how deeply connected two people are, they're bound to sometimes hurt each other with thoughtless words, selfish actions, or inconsiderate neglect. Forgiving each other for those hurtful acts is a cornerstone of any lasting, close relationship. Without forgiveness, slights and offenses accumulate like boulders on a highway. Devote yourself to clearing obstructions in your relationship through forgiveness.

> "DO NOTHING OUT OF SELFISH AMBITION OR VAIN CONCEIT. RATHER, IN HUMILITY VALUE OTHERS ABOVE YOURSELVES, NOT LOOKING TO YOUR OWN INTERESTS BUT EACH OF YOU TO THE INTERESTS OF THE OTHERS."
>
> –Philippians 2:3-4

While this may sound overly religious or metaphysical, forgiveness is, in fact, quite practical. You needn't be a saint or a mystic to pull it off. A common misconception is that to forgive someone is to let them get away with something, to call offensive or hurtful behavior okay when it plainly wasn't. The truth is, forgiveness means choosing to cancel old debts—and free yourself to get away with your heart intact, able to enjoy whatever comes next.

When you forgive, you erase grudges you've held or bad feelings you've harbored. And you create conditions for your relationship to become ever stronger. As Proverbs tells us, "One who forgives an affront fosters friendship, but one who dwells on disputes will alienate a friend" (17:9 NRSV).

17. Laugh Together

Laughing reduces stress, improves communication, gets past facades, and releases feel-good hormones in the brain. It creates great memories, helps grudges fade, and knits hearts together. Maybe your partner is always cracking you up. Or maybe neither one of you is all that funny, but you both laugh until you cry at the same movies. Wherever you find it, laughter is great for deepening connections.

The old-time comedian Victor Borge once said, "Laughter is the shortest distance between two people." Here's why: It throws open all the shutters and windows to your heart and lets your inner light shine. Give it a try—and notice how people are drawn to the warmth.

DO UNTO OTHERS AS YOU WOULD HAVE THEM DO UNTO YOU.

The Golden Rule

You've probably heard these time-honored words countless times from your parents, coaches, scout-troop leaders, and Sunday school teachers: "Do unto others as you would have them do unto you." An essential tenet at the heart of many religions (and many nonreligious groups), the Golden Rule in its simplest form urges you to treat other people the way you want to be treated.

Remember that simple and time-honored principle as you endeavor to apply the strategies I've presented above. Strive to be the kind of person you would want in a close friend. Consistently demonstrate love, trustworthiness, and compassion—and watch your relationships grow deeper and closer.

FOUR STEPS TOWARD MORE AUTHENTIC RELATIONSHIPS

Connection happens when two people are real and transparent with each other. But it can be difficult to develop authenticity in new relationships or unfamiliar situations. You may worry that your real self isn't good enough or appropriate for the situation at hand. You might also fear rejection if you are vulnerable.

So instead of being yourself, you might be tempted to present yourself as the person you think others will accept and like. Although adapting to your environment is beneficial in some situations, completely shifting your personality creates problems. People can tell if you aren't being authentic, and that limits a heart-to-heart connection.

People are attracted to authenticity. It makes them feel comfortable, safe, and respected. Here are four strategies to help you be your most authentic self:

1. **Be keenly self-aware.** As you meet new people, engage in work meetings, and spend time with different social groups, observe how you feel in each situation. Learning to be more self-aware will allow you to recognize when you are feeling uncomfortable and motivate you to act in accordance with your authentic self.

2 **Be present.** We are bombarded by distractions almost constantly, diverting our attention from the people we are with. Our minds wander, our focus shifts, our alert listening slackens. Strive to be fully present in your conversations and relationships. Be an active listener, make eye contact, and give people your full attention. Mastering the art of presence is perhaps the single most effective way to ensure authenticity in any situation.

3 **Seek to be open and vulnerable—at the proper time.** When it comes to divulging sensitive personal information, some people like to dump their problems and life story onto another person. In their eagerness to be open and honest, they might rush to bare their souls too quickly. Sharing vulnerable thoughts and feelings should happen slowly as trust is developed. Intimate aspects of our lives should be ladled out judiciously rather than dumped out hastily.

4 **Find people who share your desire for authenticity.** You can be genuine at all times and with anyone. But for a deep connection to be formed with someone, that person must also want a genuine, heart-level relationship. It's not always easy to be vulnerable with another person, but the process begins with the desire and willingness to be real together.

Connection Heals Our Hurts

What happens when you get your hand too close to a flame? Instantly, you draw your hand back. It's immediate and reactive. You get as far away from the source of the pain as you can.

This reaction to physical pain is natural. And it also can be our reaction to emotional pain. When emotionally wounded, we tend to draw back into ourselves. We become suspicious of other people. We even become suspicious of our own motives and decisions. So we withdraw—an expected and common response.

As little ones, we were wounded—perhaps by parents who didn't give us what we needed emotionally or, in the worst case, abandoned or abused us. Or maybe we were exposed to trauma. Over time, we developed patterns of relating to people based on self-protection, safety, and security. We tend to isolate, take care of ourselves, and be an island unto ourselves. Left alone in our pain, we are cut off from the healing touch that relationships can bring.

WE NEED TO BE OPEN AND HONEST WITH EACH OTHER ABOUT THE PAIN IN OUR LIVES.

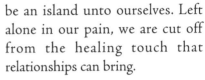

A theme woven throughout this book is that connection with others is helpful and healthy in every aspect of our lives. Our links create a close-knit community, and within that context, we can provide for the needs of others and receive help for our own necessities.

So why is it that when we need people the most, we tend to withdraw? Several factors reinforce our belief that it's better for us to be alone with our pain:

- We think others won't understand what we're going through.

- We're distrustful of others because we've been hurt by people in the past who broke our trust.

- We're unwilling to forgive those who have caused us pain.

- We're so depleted that we think we have nothing to give to another person.

- We don't believe we deserve to be loved.

Whatever reason for withdrawing, we only compound our pain by denying others the opportunity to come alongside with encouragement and support. Instead of remaining distant, we can choose to connect with others and open the doors for the healing touch we need.

We need to be open and honest with each other about the pain in our lives. We need to be willing to ask for help and support, and when asked, we need to be willing to provide it as well. By forming connections, we can exchange loneliness for companionship and participate in the double blessing of helping others to heal and being healed ourselves.

Created *for* Connection

My deep conviction that we are created for connection with others is founded on two tenets:

1. Being connected to others greatly improves our health—physically, emotionally, mentally, and spiritually.

Interpersonal connection is essential for maintaining our overall well-being. Dozens of studies have demonstrated that people who have satisfying relationships are happier, have fewer health problems, and live longer. Conversely, a lack of social ties is associated with a wide variety of mental health problems and later-life cognitive decline.

GOD WANTS EACH PERSON TO BE FULFILLED, ENJOY REWARDING RELATIONSHIPS, MAINTAIN OPTIMAL HEALTH, AND GROW INTO THEIR FULL POTENTIAL.

According to the American Psychological Association, numerous studies suggest that social isolation not only robs you of help others can give, but also has serious physical and mental consequences in itself, including elevated risk of anxiety and depression.[21]

Emma Seppälä, science director at the Stanford Center for

Compassion and Altruism Research and Education and author of *The Happiness Track*, writes,

> Studies show [that people with strong connections to others] have higher self-esteem, greater empathy for others, are more trusting and cooperative and, as a consequence, others are more open to trusting and cooperating with them. In other words, social connectedness generates a positive feedback loop of social, emotional and physical well-being. Unfortunately, the opposite is also true for those who lack social connectedness. Low levels of social connection are associated with declines in physical and psychological health as well as a higher likelihood for antisocial behavior that leads to further isolation.[22]

2. God created people to be connected to others—so we can live the abundant life he intended for us.

As a person of faith, I am convinced that God wants each person to be fulfilled, enjoy rewarding relationships, maintain optimal health, and grow into their full potential. A key way he enables us to achieve each of these is through meaningful and supportive relationships.

Aside from a close relationship with God himself, there is nothing like strong connections with friends and loved ones to help us experience life with maximum joy, contentment, and wellness. This is why Scripture is teeming with verses like these:

- "Two are better than one, because they have a good return for their labor: If either of them falls down, one can help the other up. But pity anyone who falls and has no one to help them up" (Ecclesiastes 4:9–10).

- "A friend is always loyal, and a brother is born to help in time of need" (Proverbs 17:17 NLT).

- "The heartfelt counsel of a friend is as sweet as perfume and incense" (Proverbs 27:9 NLT).

- "As iron sharpens iron, so one person sharpens another" (Proverbs 27:17).

This list could go on and on, because God knows we need close connection with others to thrive and grow into the people he created us to become.

Hope Is *a* Powerful Ally

Other factors are also essential to achieve deep connections, such as wise guidance, courage to step out of your comfort zone, and the willingness to develop new skills. But I believe hope is the indispensable quality that allows you to overcome fear, muster motivation, and press forward to a bright future.

In three decades as a mental health expert, I have counseled thousands of people who needed help coping with pain and fear of every kind: anxiety, depression, guilt, anger, addiction, and the emotional scars of physical and psychological abuse. Through those years of coming alongside clients as they courageously sought to address their struggles, I have seen countless times that *hope* is a key ingredient to healing. My team and I adopted Jeremiah 29:11–14 as our clinic's guiding Scripture passage:

HOPE IS THE INDISPENSABLE QUALITY THAT ALLOWS YOU TO OVERCOME FEAR, MUSTER MOTIVATION, AND PRESS FORWARD TO A BRIGHT FUTURE.

"I know the plans I have for you," declares the LORD, "plans to prosper you and not to harm you, plans to give you hope and a future. Then you will call on me and come and pray to me, and I will listen to you. You will seek me and find me when you seek me with all your heart. I will be found by you," declares the LORD, "and will bring you back from captivity."

I encourage you to reflect on these life-changing words and embrace them as your touchstone as you pursue your own emotional, spiritual, and physical wellness. Hopefulness will . . .

- Renew your motivation to reach out to new people.

- Replenish your energy to invest in relationships with authenticity and openness.

- Reboot your imagination and dreams for the life you've been longing for, full of loving people who will build you up.

TEN WAYS TO BE A GREAT FRIEND

It's said that the quality of our lives is largely determined by the quality of our friendships. Your traveling companions on the journey of life can pick you up when you fall, bring out your best, and propel you forward.

The surest way to have great friendships is to be a great friend. Here are simple yet powerful ways to be just that:

1. **Build trust.** For all relationships—friends, lovers, coworkers—consistent demonstrations of trustworthiness form the bond that holds people together.

2. **Be there.** Show up, physically and emotionally, for your friend's important events (and unimportant ones too).

3. **Practice positivity.** Optimism beats pessimism hands down—and your friend will benefit from your upbeat attitude.

4. **Initiate consistently.** Don't wait for the other person to text or call you—take the initiative yourself.

5. **Affirm differences.** Celebrate the other person's unique perspective, even if it conflicts with your own.

6 **Give generously.** Pick up the tab, send a gift for no reason, offer to help move. A generous spirit will come back to you in unexpected ways.

7 **Peel the onion.** Make the effort to dig deep into the other person's life to discover what lies below the surface.

8 **Accept the ebb and flow.** Friendships go through times of closeness and times of distance. Stay committed throughout.

9 **Apologize when you blow it.** A sincere apology is the quickest and surest way to smooth over rough patches.

10 **Create new memories.** Meeting at the same old coffee shop to catch up is fine, but friendships are deepened through shared adventure and discovery.

Notes

1   "Cigna Takes Action to Combat the Rise of Loneliness and
    Improve Mental Wellness in America," *Cigna Newsroom*. Last
    updated January 23, 2020. *https://www.cigna.com/about-us/
    newsroom/news-and-views/press-releases/2020/cigna-takes
    -action-to-combat-the-rise-of-loneliness-and-improve-mental
    -wellness-in-america* (March 3, 3022).

2   Debra Umberson and Jennifer Karas Montez, "Social
    Relationships and Health: A Flashpoint for Health Policy,"
    *NCBI. https://www.ncbi.nlm.nih.gov/pmc/articles/
    PMC3150158/* (March 3, 2022).

3   "KFF/Economist Survey: One in Five Americans
    Report Always or Often Feeling Lonely or Socially
    Isolated, Frequently with Physical, Mental, and Financial
    Consequences," *Kaiser Family Foundation/KFF Newsroom*.
    Last updated August 31, 2018. *https://www.kff.org/other/
    press-release/survey-one-in-five-americans-report-loneliness
    -social-isolation* (March 3, 2022).

4   Richard Weissbourd, et al., "Loneliness in America: How
    the Pandemic Has Deepened an Epidemic of Loneliness and

What We Can Do about It," *Harvard Graduate School of Education, Making Caring Common Project.* https://static1.squarespace.com/static/5b7c56e255b02c683659fe43/t/6021776bdd04957c4557c212/1612805995893/Loneliness+in+America+2021_02_08_FINAL.pdf (March 8, 2022).

5   "Loneliness in America," *Harvard Graduate School of Education.*

6   "Loneliness and the Workplace," *Cigna.com.* https://www.cigna.com/static/www-cigna-com/docs/about-us/newsroom/studies-and-reports/combatting-loneliness/cigna-2020-loneliness-factsheet.pdf (March 3, 2022).

7   Stephanie Cacioppo et al., "Loneliness: Clinical Import and Interventions," *Perspectives on Psychological Science* 10, no. 2 (March 11, 2015): 143–44.

8   Martina Advaney, "To Talk or Not to Talk[—]That Is the Question!" *Youth Time.* Last updated May 6, 2017. https://youth-time.eu/to-talk-or-not-to-talk-that-is-the-question-at-least-70-percent-of-communication-is-non-verbal/ (March 11, 2022).

9   Cody Kommers, "Which Is Better: More Friends or Closer Friends?" *Psychology Today.* Last updated September 11, 2018. https://www.psychologytoday.com/us/blog/friendly-interest/201809/which-is-better-more-friends-or-closer-friends (March 3, 2022).

10 "What Do We Mean by Personal Relationships?" *University of Minnesota, Taking Charge of Your Health & Wellbeing.* https://www.takingcharge.csh.umn.edu/what-do-we-mean-personal-relationships (March 3, 2022).

11 "Loneliness in America," *Harvard Graduate School of Education.*

12 Dan Buettner, *Thrive: Finding Happiness the Blue Zones Way* (Washington, DC: National Geographic Society, 2011), 224.

13 Steven W. Cole, "Social Regulation of Human Gene Expression: Mechanisms and Implications for Public Health," *American Journal of Public Health* 103, suppl. 1 (October 2013): S84–S92.

14 "The Health Benefits of Strong Relationships," *Harvard Health Publishing, Harvard Medical School.* Last updated December 1, 2010. *https://www.health.harvard.edu/ newsletter_article/the-health-benefits-of-strong-relationships* (March 3, 2022).

15 Kendra Cherry, "Loneliness: Causes and Health Consequences," *Verywell Mind.* Last updated September 1, 2021. *https://www.verywellmind.com/loneliness-causes-effects -and-treatments-2795749* (March 3, 2022).

16 Max Lucado, *Traveling Light: Releasing the Burdens You Were Never Intended to Bear* (Nashville: W Publishing Group, 2001), 77.

17 Jacqueline Olds and Richard Schwartz, *The Lonely American* (Boston: Beacon Press, 2009), 1.

18 "Loneliness in America," *Harvard Graduate School of Education.*

19 Sherry Amatenstein, "Not So Social Media: How Social Media Increases Loneliness," *Psycom.net. https://www .psycom.net/how-social-media-increases-loneliness/* (March 3, 2022).

20 David Niven, *100 Simple Secrets of Great Relationships* (San Francisco: HarperOne, 2006), 37.

21 Amy Novotney, "The Risks of Social Isolation," *American Psychological Association* 50, no. 5 (May 2019): 32.

22 Emma Seppälä, "Connectedness & Health: The Science of Social Connection," *Stanford Medicine, The Center for Compassion and Altruism Research and Education. http://ccare.stanford.edu/uncategorized/connectedness-health-the-science-of-social-connection-infographic/* (March 3, 2022).

Image Credits

Images used under license from (1) **Shutterstock.com**: r.classen, cover and pp. 3, 5, 11, 29, 51, 71, 97, 107; Rido, pp. 6, 36; nadia_if, p. 7; fizkes, pp. 8, 69, 90, 98; Prostock-studio, p. 9; insta_photos, p. 10; Pixel-Shot, p. 12; Runrun2, p. 13; didesign021, p. 15; Dmitry Demidovich, p. 22; Tero Vesalainen, p. 25; BigPixel Photo, p. 26; KieferPix, pp. 31, 100; SewCream, p. 32; Syda Productions, p. 35; Zoran Pucarevic, p. 39; GAS-photo, p. 43; Alex Ghidan, p. 44; Lee Yiu Tung, p. 55; KREUS, p. 57; guruXOX, p. 58; asiandelight, p. 63; New Africa, p. 64; Nesolenaya Alexandra, p. 65; Monkey Business Images, pp. 66, 78; Flamingo Images, p. 73; peampath2812, p. 77; SFIO CRACHO, p. 79; Rawpixel.com, p. 83; Natalya Erofeeva, p. 87; Dmytro Zinkevych, p. 93; Robert Kneschke, p. 99; Pop Tika, p. 103; Syda Productions, p. 104; and (2) **Unsplash**: Helena Lopes, p. 19.

MORE RESOURCES FROM DR. GREGORY L. JANTZ

Unmasking Emotional Abuse	**Five Keys to Health and Healing**
Six Steps to Reduce Stress	**40 Answers for Teens' Top Questions**
Ten Tips for Parenting the Smartphone Generation	**When a Loved One Is Addicted**
Five Keys to Dealing with Depression	**Social Media and Depression**
Seven Answers for Anxiety	**Rebuilding Trust after Betrayal**
Five Keys to Raising Boys	**How to Deal with Toxic People**
Freedom From Shame	**The Power of Connection**

www.hendricksonrose.com